The Art of Thinking

A BK Publications Book

First Publication 2000

ISBN 1-886872-20-1

Published by the Brahma Kumaris Information Services, Ltd. Global Co-operation House, 65 Pound Lane, London NW10 2HH, UK

Printed by Leighton Printing, London, UK

Contents

MIND MAPS

For most people today, more information than ever before is available about the world around us. Nevertheless, we often grow up with only a limited understanding and awareness of the world inside us - our thoughts, feelings, attitudes and emotions. Even when we do take a closer look at some of these internal goings-on, we tend to feel that they are largely dictated by external events. However that need not be so. Improved knowledge of the deeper self, and the inner landscape over which the mind ranges, can immeasurably improve the quality of life's journey, providing orientation, widening horizons and opening up new directions. Mind Maps is a series of short spiritual guides to help the traveller along the way.

Introduction

The basis for the art of thinking is the art of living and the basis for the art of living is the art of thinking. Whatever my thoughts, that is what I become. We achieve our dreams and aspirations on the basis of our own thinking.

If I want to make my life full of truth and beauty, then let my thoughts be full of truth and beauty. This sounds very simple but our thoughts are rather like a ball of mercury, difficult to capture.

The mind moves in a thousand different directions and at great speed. Sometimes we don't know where it is going or why, and only after the experience do we begin to see what has happened. Then we say, "Why did that happen?" We don't realise that it is I myself who made it happen or allowed it to happen.

Personal Responsibility

PERSONAL RESPONSIBILITY

If something happens which we don't like, very often the human tendency is to point 'out there'. Gandhi made the famous observation that if you point one finger outwards, you are actually pointing three fingers towards yourself! Try it! This little gesture is an indicator that when I start thinking that what's happening 'out there' is responsible for my experience, I need to remind myself that I am the creator of my own thoughts and responses. I am responsible for what is happening in my inner world. I am responsible for my own state of peace, well-being, happiness and love. It is not somebody or something else that is responsible for any of these things.

In good times responsibility can be very sweet, but I also have to accept responsibility when I am going through an unhappy time. To accept the

responsibility that this is what I have done to myself can be quite painful, yet the art of thinking makes me realise that when I do not take responsibility for what is happening inside, I allow the things outside to influence me. And it is when I allow external situations and people to affect me that I no longer have control over the quality of my experience. At this present time much of what is going on in the world is not

filled with truth and beauty. So, of course, if I simply open myself to react to everything that is happening around me, then what happens to me inside is not going to be very comfortable nor very beautiful. Realising my responsibility, I am challenged to make a decision whether to take on all that negativity or rather to respond creatively with positive thoughts and responses from my own inner world.

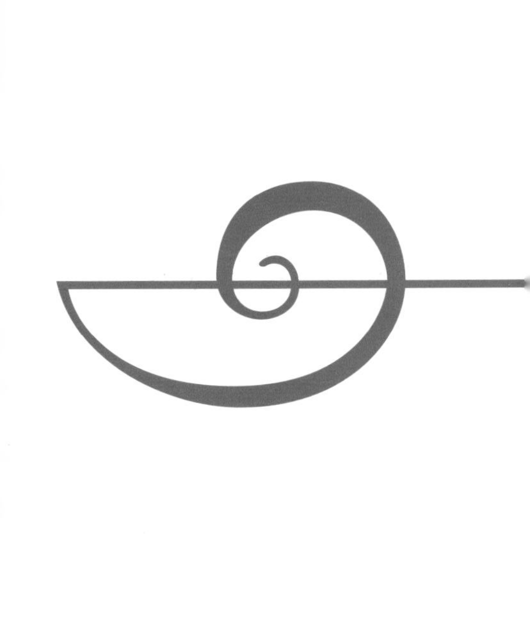

Detachment

DETACHMENT

Where do I begin? I can begin with detachment. This is a word that is very much mis-understood. Detachment doesn't mean cutting off. It doesn't mean running away. It means learning to separate two different things, the world outside and the world inside, and being able to see these worlds as separate.

Outside are my job, study, finances, relationships, etc. Inside are the subtle things that are less easily measured, things that are non-physical - my feelings, emotions, conscience, consciousness and personality - all of which happen in my inner world, within my own spiritual identity. These are the ingredients which I, the detached observer, can creatively experiment with in the 'art' of thinking and can use in the art of living.

Mind
&
Spirit

Mind and spirit

In the traditional understanding of spirituality mind and spirit are often seen as separate. But I would suggest that the mind is part of my spirituality. With the awareness of myself as a spiritual being, I can go deeper and deeper, through the level of conscious thought to the level of feelings, motives and conscience. With this awareness, I begin to create

thoughts on that deeper level. As I consciously look at what is happening in my mind, i.e. as I observe the quality of my thinking and understand where it is coming from, then I start to be selective. As a detached observer, I choose which types of thoughts I would like to have. I am responsible for whatever thoughts I create. What I will become totally depends on what types of thoughts I choose to have. So the art of

thinking starts with the ability to stand back and look inside my own mind.

This practice of standing back and looking inside my mind is a very powerful and fruitful exercise, but if I don't take the time and trouble to do this for myself, then what usually happens is that life just pushes me around, because I have not decided on my direction myself. Standing back and observing what is happening

in my mind enables me to choose my own destination and to decide what steps to take to make things happen. This process involves the clear separation of all external factors from what is happening within my inner world. Naturally, I continue to give the right attention to the external situation, but only when I see this separation can I really look at what is happening in my inner world. What feelings and emotions

are arising? Where do these feelings and emotions come from? I begin to see that these are very much connected with my own pattern of thinking.

Changing my Thought Patterns

Changing my thought patterns

If I develop the skill of separating things outside from things inside, then I begin to see the particular patterns or thought cycles which go on inside myself and I notice how they allow certain feelings and emotions to arise. For how long have I been carrying these feelings that I am reacting with today?

I can probably trace them back to my childhood. If I always do something a certain way, it becomes a habit so that I don't even realise that I'm doing it.

I automatically react to the situation, and my internal reaction in turn prompts the external action. For example, I may open the garage doors for the car every day and so still open the garage doors even though that day the car is parked somewhere else! Once

we have performed the same action two or three times it is well on the way to becoming a habit. The same type of automatic responses happen with my thought patterns, although at a deeper and less obvious level.

Here is a little experiment. Take a sheet of paper and put a dot in the middle. Ask people what they see. Most people will say they see 'a dot'. The reality is that 99% of the sheet is blank, but people won't notice that. They will comment on the one little dot. We may have the habit of seeing people like this. 99% of a person is positive, but he or she will have one little flaw, and that is what we react to. It is unrecognised habits like this that create my feelings, my emotions and my thoughts, as well as my behaviour.

To start to work on those things deep within my own being takes time, effort and

courage, particularly in today's world where our energy is being pulled in so many different directions. Human souls have lost spiritual power and energy. To regain power, I have to refocus and redirect the energy of my mind.

Once I am aware that I am actually creating my own thoughts, then I can begin to study and master the art of creating the best thoughts, thoughts which I understand

are good thoughts. For example, instead of reacting to the flaws in others, I can practise looking for their special qualities and virtues, until eventually this practice becomes a new habit. Positive thoughts and thought habits like this are going to bring benefit to me and other people.

Sometimes we think that it is an 'either/or' situation, that I must choose between benefit to me or benefit to someone

else, but that is not so. Something damaging or dangerous for me will also have an impact on others. If there is something which is powerful and truly beneficial to me then the benefit that I have gained will be a resource available for me to use for the benefit of all around me.

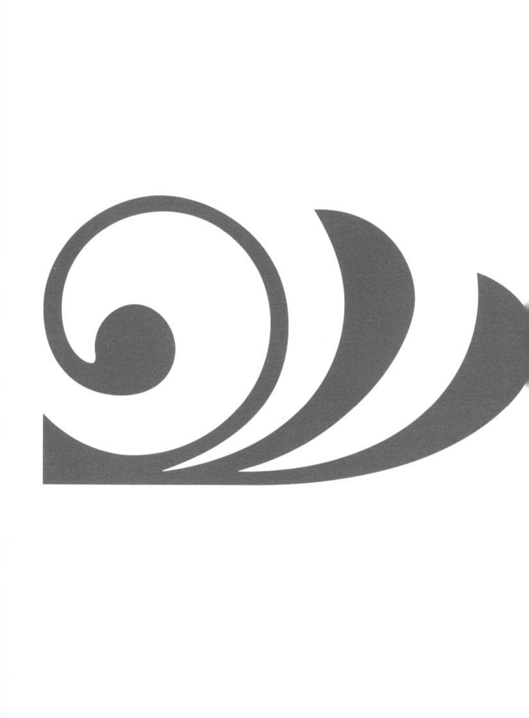

Thinking as an Art

THINKING AS AN ART

The word 'art' sometimes implies a God-given gift, but, regardless of its origin, a work of art usually has to be nurtured, developed and refined by the artist. So too with the art of thinking. We all are blessed with the ability to create thoughts, i.e. we can think! However, making the art of thinking powerful, to enable ourselves to experience goodness in life and share that

with others, requires a process of training and discipline. I myself, the spiritual being, train and discipline my own mind.

Just as art truly flourishes against the backdrop of a certain quality of culture, in the same way, the right company, atmosphere and study are all necessary to develop my art of thinking. In the early days of this self training it is very helpful to be

able to share and connect with others who are engaged in a similar process, in order to harness the necessary power.

Later on, in this fascinating journey, I will probably be able to manage without the additional input from others because by then the internal power I have developed will enable me to withstand any contradictory forces.

Taking Responsibility

Taking responsibility

If we don't take this responsibility, or are not aware of how to develop this art, generally our deepest, most constant feelings are not of peace or happiness. For example, when did you last wake up with the thought that this is a wonderful life? If I were to walk down the streets of most large cities on any day of the week, I could probably count on the fingers of one

hand the number of faces that actually radiate the joy of life.

I think that the natural state of the human spirit is joy, truth and beauty, but somehow we have moved very far away from that state. This situation should send a signal to us that the art of thinking has been forgotten and the art of living has somehow been lost.

Another simple, practical experiment can be of help

here. Sit quietly and create a memory of a brilliant sunset, a host of daffodils in spring or some other beautiful memory of your choice. Hold this image in your mind and experience it. The feelings evoked are not artificial. They are real. You have simply re-created an image, in your own mind, that has triggered certain feelings and emotions which are absolutely real. You don't even have to work very hard at it.

This shows how powerful thoughts can be and how using imagery and visualisation works in relation to feelings and emotions. When I have decided what types of thoughts to have, then, within my own being, I can begin to create those feelings that I would like to have.

Challenges

Challenges

When I take on the responsibility for my own thoughts, I may find that I am challenged, not only by old habits but also by my own body. For example, if I sit and create the feeling of peace, I may be pulled by pain or discomfort that arises in my body for one reason or another. But if I remember that although the mind and the body are interconnected

they are also separate, then I can hold on to my feelings of peace and even heal the body at the same time by sending vibrations of peace to it.

We are also challenged by situations. When my father was very ill I had to spend long hours for several days waiting in a hospital corridor. Everyone around seemed so very busy and stressed. I consciously started to send out vibrations of peace and when we do this a sweet smile naturally comes to the face. Before long, people were smiling back at me and the atmosphere had lightened. So I knew that the thought vibrations were having an impact on others, although everyone was just as busy as before.

Positively dealing with the challenges of body and circumstances actually helps us in developing the art of thinking.

Cause
&
Effect

Cause and effect

Relationships are perhaps the most intense of all the external factors that we have to deal with in life. I would like to introduce a word and concept from the spiritual vocabulary: 'karma'. Most people are familiar with this word but there are a variety of mis-conceptions about it. In fact, the word 'karma' simply means 'action' and as a concept it refers to

the principle of action and reaction, the law that every cause produces an effect.

In relationships, that principle relates to giving and taking, receiving and sharing. According to this law of give and take, once I decide what state of inner being I want to maintain, that state becomes the seed or cause that I will also bring into my relationships. What I am inside is what I will project

through my give and take in relationships, whether I want to or not. And what I give is what will come back to me.

So taking the responsibility to change my own thoughts and feelings can radically shift the balance in relationships and transform them.

Empowering my Effort

EMPOWERING MY EFFORT

Finally, I would like to share how the art of thinking can be empowered. In my spiritual awareness, mind and spirit are not separate but are together. The mind is not lower than the spirit, but is a part of it. I, the spirit, go through ups and downs and all sorts of phases and stages - good, not so good and coming back to good again.

The spirit goes through these cyclical patterns and the thoughts that arise in the mind simply reflect the quality of the spirit itself. If I choose the thoughts that I would like to have, and pay attention to maintaining them, I am actually transforming the state of the spirit and my own overall state of being. One of the spiritual aims of life's journey is to re-experience the original state of the spirit.

When the mind is full of rubbish it is impossible to feel this original pure state, but if we start to clean the mind then the original virtues of the spirit will emerge.

In my experience, there is another step I can take - beyond just paying attention to my mind - that will help me along the way. I actually focus my thoughts on the Supreme Soul, the spiritual Source, and allow that influence to work on

me, the spirit. I make this link or connection through the practice of meditation and also by reminding myself of it whenever possible throughout the day. This aids and empowers my effort. It is like the rays of the sun touching a seed, with the result that whatever is latent in the seed begins to grow and then bloom.

So on one level I am working on my mind and thoughts, whilst on another level I am

allowing the light of the Supreme to clean me, the spirit, and emerge that which is within me.

On a third level, I am paying attention to my lifestyle and my actions throughout the day. If my actions are good, then that is going to have an impact on my mind. And if my mind is full of goodness, then that is going to direct and influence my life. This is a cycle in which the

increasingly positive state of my mind has a beneficial influence on my life as a whole, while a life filled with goodness allows the mind to move more easily in the direction of truth and beauty.

About the Author

B.K. Jayanti is a spiritual teacher and leader, a gifted meditator and an emissary for peace. She has a vision and experience that is truly global and deeply spiritual. Born in India of Sindhi parents, who migrated to England when she was eight years old, she is a blend of Eastern wisdom and Western education and culture.

At the age of 19 she embarked on a journey of spiritual study and service with the Brahma Kumaris World Spiritual University, and at the age of 21, decided to dedicate her life to this path. She has spent over 30 years in the company of some of the world's most remarkable yogis, gleaning much of their wisdom and insights. As a result, she herself is an extraordinary meditator and teacher and has developed a clarity and purity of mind that is exceptional. B.K. Jayanti is also a much sought-after speaker around the world.

Her natural wisdom and gentle, though powerful, personality have touched and inspired hundreds of thousands of people. She is the European Director of the Brahma Kumaris World Spiritual University and assists in co-ordinating the University's activities in more than 70 countries. She is also its main representative to the United Nations, Geneva.

Mind Map series of booklets on topics of practical spirituality is based on talks and lectures given by teachers of the Brahma Kumaris World Spiritual University.

About the Brahma Kumaris

The Brahma Kumaris World Spiritual University is an international organisation working at all levels of society for positive change. Established in 1937 it now carries out a wide range of educational programmes for the development of human and spiritual values throughout its 4000 centres in over 70 countries.

The University is a non-governmental organisation in general consultative status with the Economic and Social Council of the United Nations and in consultative status with UNICEF. It is also the recipient of seven UN Peace Messenger Awards.

Locally, centres provide courses and lectures in meditation and positive values, enabling individuals to recognise their true potential and make the most of their lives. The University offers all its services free of charge.

INTERNATIONAL HEADQUARTERS

PO BOX No 2, MOUNT ABU, RAJASTHAN 307501, INDIA

Tel: (+91) 2974 38261-68 Fax: (+91) 2974 38952

E-mail: bkabu@vsnl.com

INTERNATIONAL CO-ORDINATING OFFICE & REGIONAL OFFICE FOR EUROPE AND THE MIDDLE EAST

Global Co-operation House, 65 Pound Lane, London, NW10 2HH, UK

Tel: (+44) 020 8727 3350 Fax: (+44) 020 8727 3351

E-mail: london@bkwsu.com

AFRICA

Global Museum for a Better World, Maua Close, off Parklands Road, Westlands, PO Box 12349, Nairobi, Kenya

Tel: (+254) 2 743 572 Fax: (+254) 2 743 885

E-mail: bkwsugm@holidaybazaar.com

AUSTRALIA AND EAST ASIA

78 Alt Street, Ashfield, Sydney, NSW 2131, Australia

Tel: (+61) 2 9716 7066 Fax: (+61) 2 9716 7795

E-mail: indra@one.net.au

NORTH AND SOUTH AMERICAS AND THE CARIBBEAN

Global Harmony House, 46 S. Middle Neck Road, Great Neck, NY 11021, USA
Tel: (+1) 516 773 0971 Fax: (+1) 516 773 0976
E-mail: newyork@bkwsu.com

RUSSIA AND CIS

Angels' House 2, Gospitalnaya Ploschad., Build 1, Moscow 111020, Russia
Tel: (+7) 095 263 02 47 Fax: (+7) 095 261 32 24
E-mail: bkwsu@mail.ru

www.bkwsu.com

www.bkpublications.com

e-mail enquiries@bkpublications.com